Dorsal fin of a lemon shark

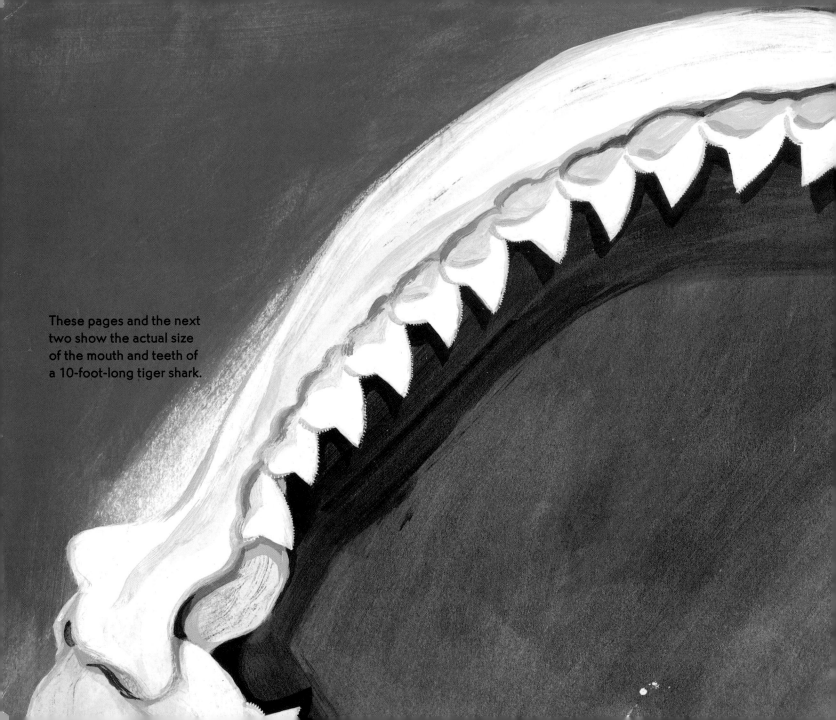

These pages and the next two show the actual size of the mouth and teeth of a 10-foot-long tiger shark.

ALL ABOUT SHARKS

JIM ARNOSKY

Scholastic Press • New York

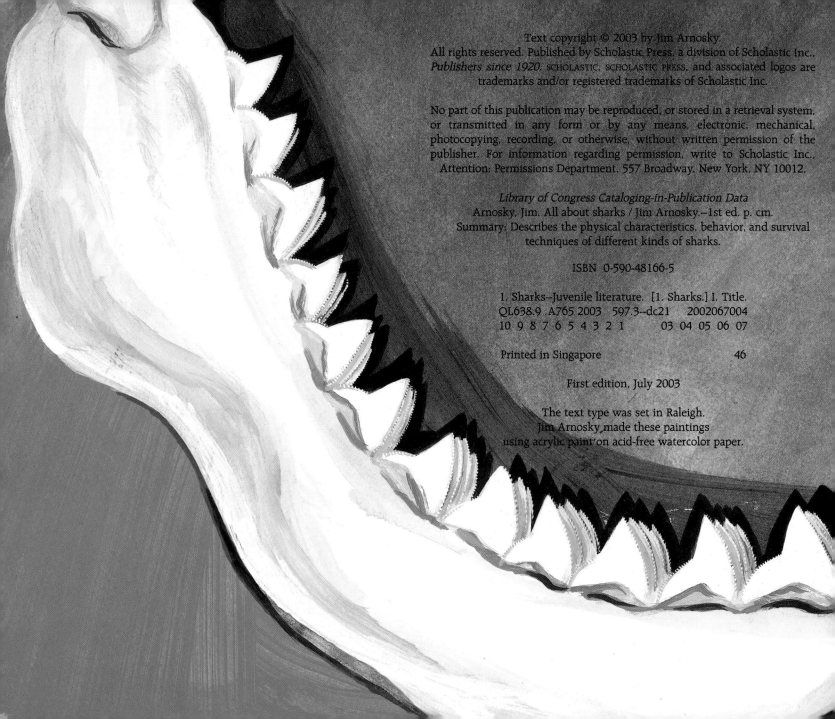

Library of Congress Cataloging-in-Publication Data
Arnosky, Jim. All about sharks / Jim Arnosky.--1st ed. p. cm.
Summary: Describes the physical characteristics, behavior, and survival
techniques of different kinds of sharks.

ISBN 0-590-48166-5

1. Sharks--Juvenile literature. [1. Sharks.] I. Title.
QL638.9 .A765 2003   597.3--dc21   2002067004
10 9 8 7 6 5 4 3 2 1   03 04 05 06 07

Printed in Singapore   46

First edition, July 2003

The text type was set in Raleigh.
Jim Arnosky made these paintings
using acrylic paint on acid-free watercolor paper.

For Heidi

Have you ever wondered about sharks?
How big do they grow?
How sharp are their teeth?
What do they eat?
Why do they attack people?

This book answers all of
these questions and more.
It's all about sharks!

Sharks have been swimming in the oceans for millions of years, and they haven't changed much in all that time. Like their prehistoric ancestors, today's sharks are predators that feed on other living things.

Mako shark

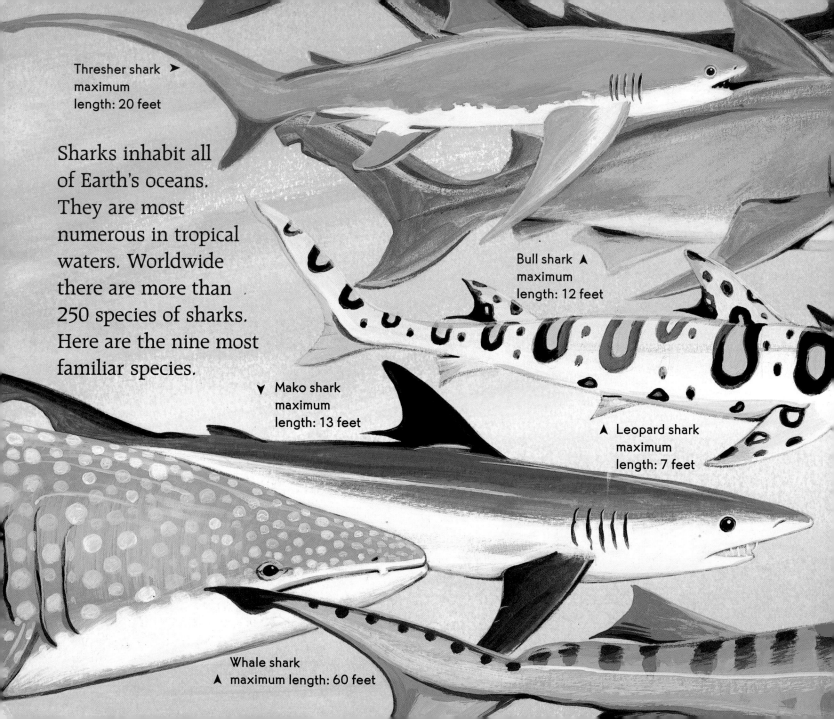

Thresher shark ➤
maximum
length: 20 feet

Sharks inhabit all
of Earth's oceans.
They are most
numerous in tropical
waters. Worldwide
there are more than
250 species of sharks.
Here are the nine most
familiar species.

Bull shark ▲
maximum
length: 12 feet

▼ Mako shark
maximum
length: 13 feet

▲ Leopard shark
maximum
length: 7 feet

Whale shark
▲ maximum length: 60 feet

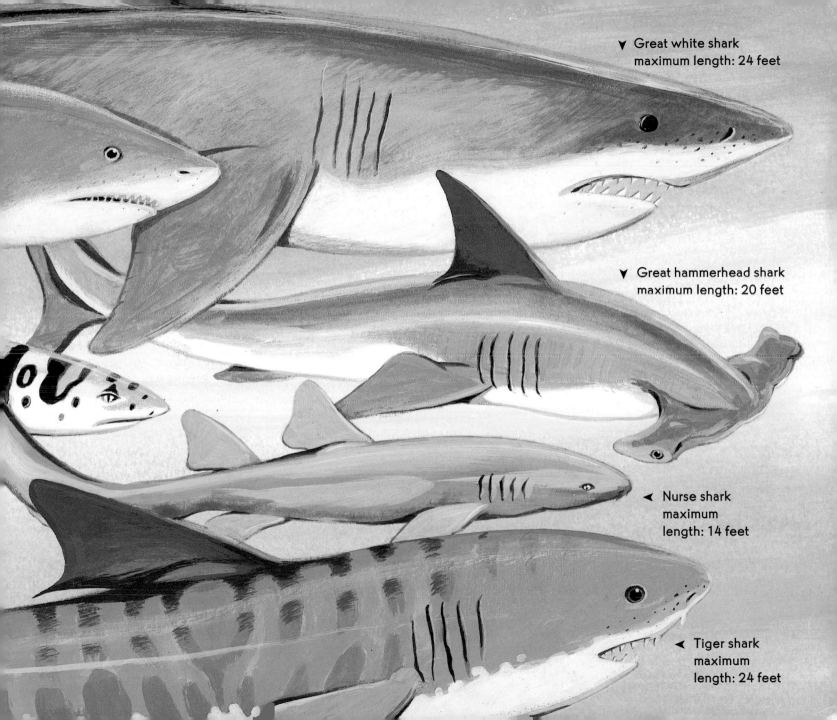

▼ Great white shark
maximum length: 24 feet

▼ Great hammerhead shark
maximum length: 20 feet

◄ Nurse shark
maximum
length: 14 feet

◄ Tiger shark
maximum
length: 24 feet

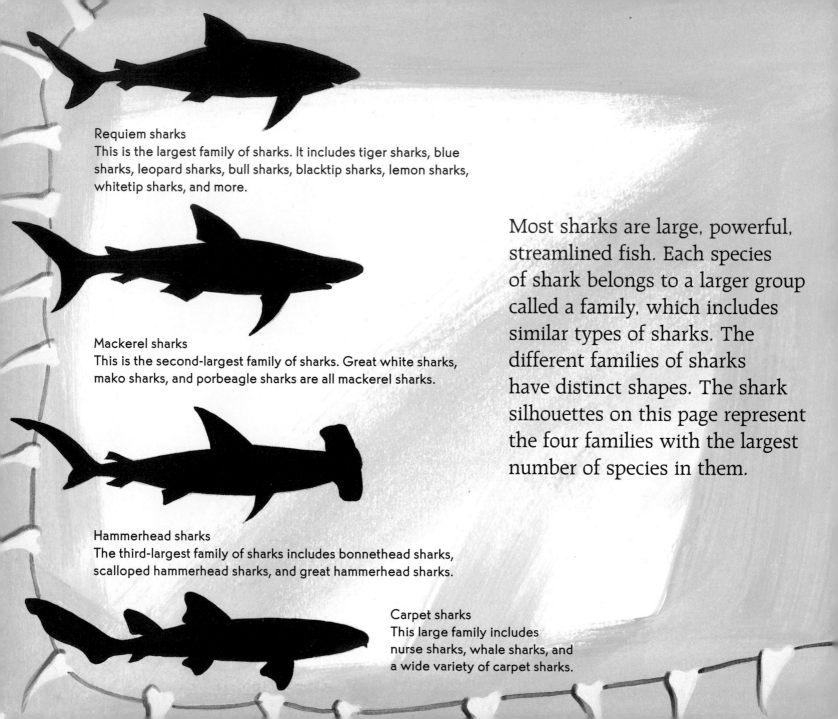

Requiem sharks
This is the largest family of sharks. It includes tiger sharks, blue sharks, leopard sharks, bull sharks, blacktip sharks, lemon sharks, whitetip sharks, and more.

Mackerel sharks
This is the second-largest family of sharks. Great white sharks, mako sharks, and porbeagle sharks are all mackerel sharks.

Hammerhead sharks
The third-largest family of sharks includes bonnethead sharks, scalloped hammerhead sharks, and great hammerhead sharks.

Carpet sharks
This large family includes nurse sharks, whale sharks, and a wide variety of carpet sharks.

Most sharks are large, powerful, streamlined fish. Each species of shark belongs to a larger group called a family, which includes similar types of sharks. The different families of sharks have distinct shapes. The shark silhouettes on this page represent the four families with the largest number of species in them.

The two most unusually shaped sharks are horn sharks and angel sharks. Horn sharks resemble the earliest-known sharks. Angel sharks have very flat bodies.

Horn sharks are bottom-dwellers that feed primarily on shellfish.

Angel sharks are also bottom-feeders. Like stingrays, they can hide by partially burying themselves in sand.

Sharks do not have bones. Their skeletons are made entirely of cartilage, the same flexible material that gives shape to human ears and noses. A shark's body is so limber it can bend around and bite its tail.

Parts of a Typical Shark

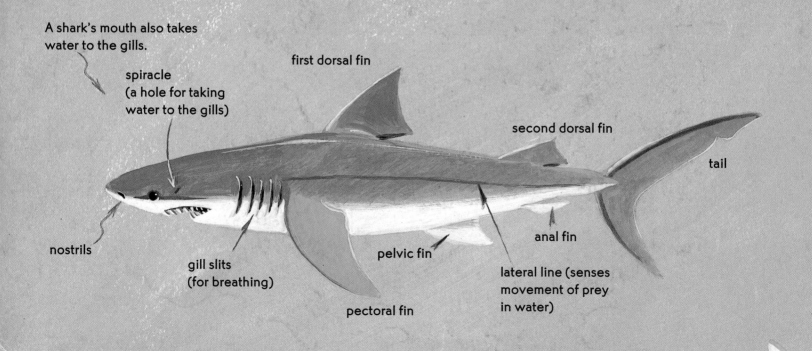

A shark's mouth also takes water to the gills.

spiracle (a hole for taking water to the gills)

first dorsal fin

second dorsal fin

tail

nostrils

gill slits (for breathing)

pelvic fin

anal fin

lateral line (senses movement of prey in water)

pectoral fin

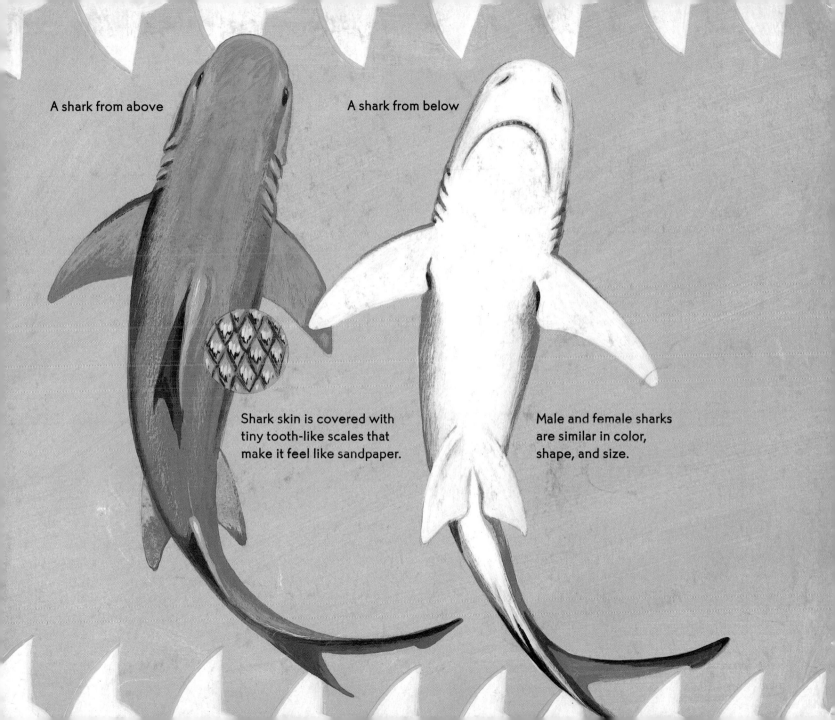

A shark from above

A shark from below

Shark skin is covered with tiny tooth-like scales that make it feel like sandpaper.

Male and female sharks are similar in color, shape, and size.

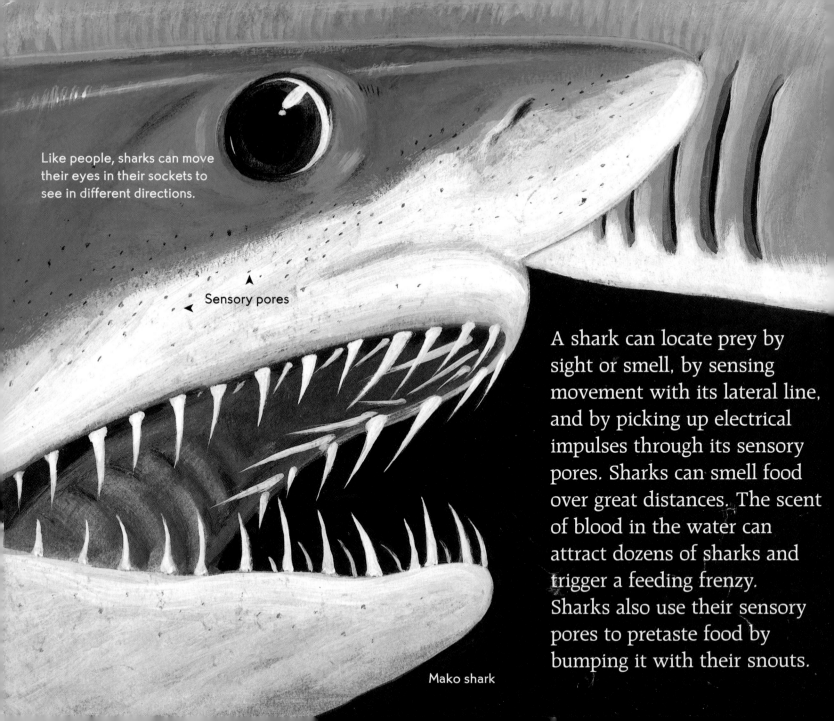

Like people, sharks can move their eyes in their sockets to see in different directions.

Sensory pores

A shark can locate prey by sight or smell, by sensing movement with its lateral line, and by picking up electrical impulses through its sensory pores. Sharks can smell food over great distances. The scent of blood in the water can attract dozens of sharks and trigger a feeding frenzy. Sharks also use their sensory pores to pretaste food by bumping it with their snouts.

Mako shark

Great hammerhead shark

Lateral line ▼

Sand shark

Hammerhead shark eyes are positioned on the ends of their wide hammer-shaped heads. This gives hammerheads better distance perception than other sharks.

Sharks have no eyelids. But many species of sharks have movable, transparent, nictitating membranes that cover and protect the sharks' eyes when attacking and eating.

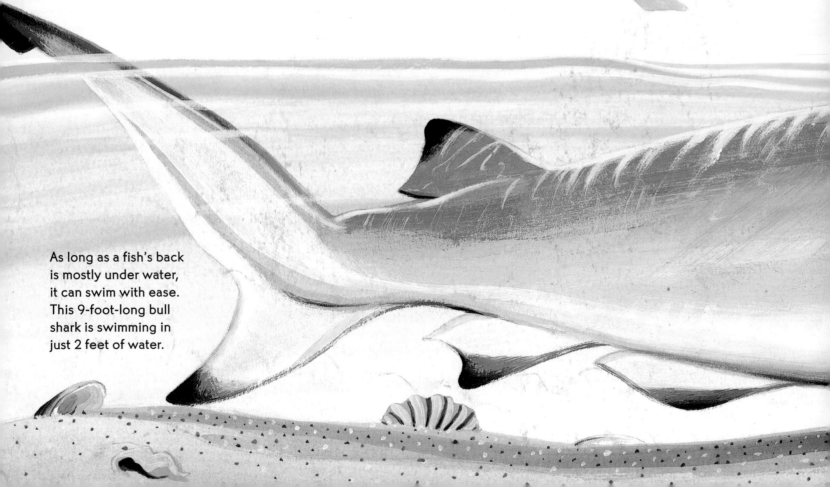

Most shark attacks on people occur in shallow water. There is a reason for this. Breaking waves near the shore scoop out the sandy bottom and create gullies. Schools of fish swim in the gullies, and large fish, including sharks, come to feed on them. These gullies are often only a few feet away from the beach. Considering how often sharks swim close to shore, shark attacks on people are amazingly rare.

As long as a fish's back is mostly under water, it can swim with ease. This 9-foot-long bull shark is swimming in just 2 feet of water.

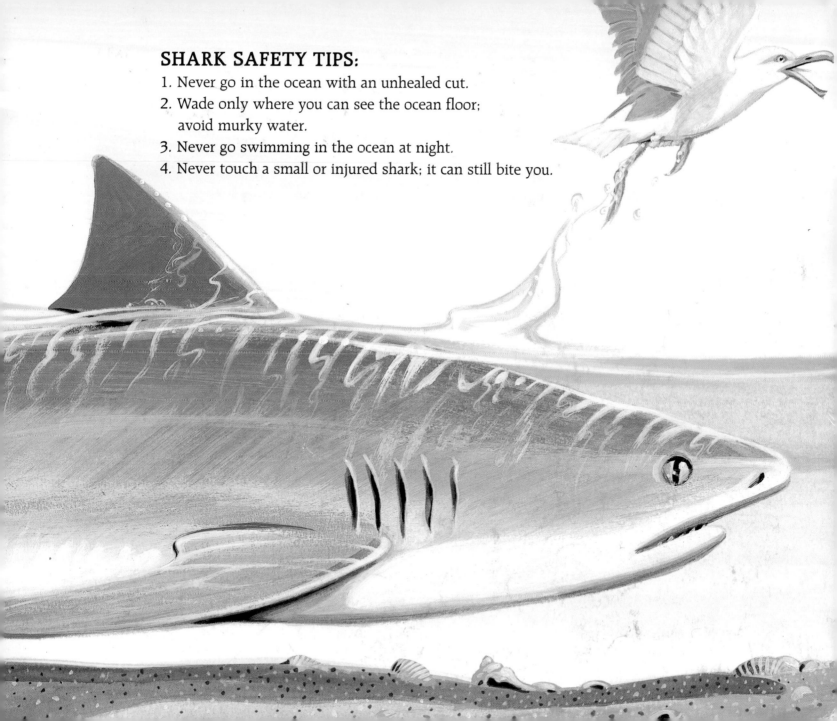

SHARK SAFETY TIPS:

1. Never go in the ocean with an unhealed cut.
2. Wade only where you can see the ocean floor; avoid murky water.
3. Never go swimming in the ocean at night.
4. Never touch a small or injured shark; it can still bite you.

With its mouth situated on the underside of its head, how does a shark bite something out in front of it?

By temporarily dislocating its jaw and jutting it forward. That's how!

When a shark takes a big bite, it bites with more than 300 razor-sharp teeth.

Sharks have 40-45 front teeth, with up to 7 rows of replacement teeth behind them. The replacement teeth move forward whenever a front tooth breaks or becomes worn and falls out. It takes about one day for a replacement tooth to move forward and take its position in the shark's front row of teeth.

Great white shark

This side view of a shark's teeth shows the replacement teeth behind a front tooth.

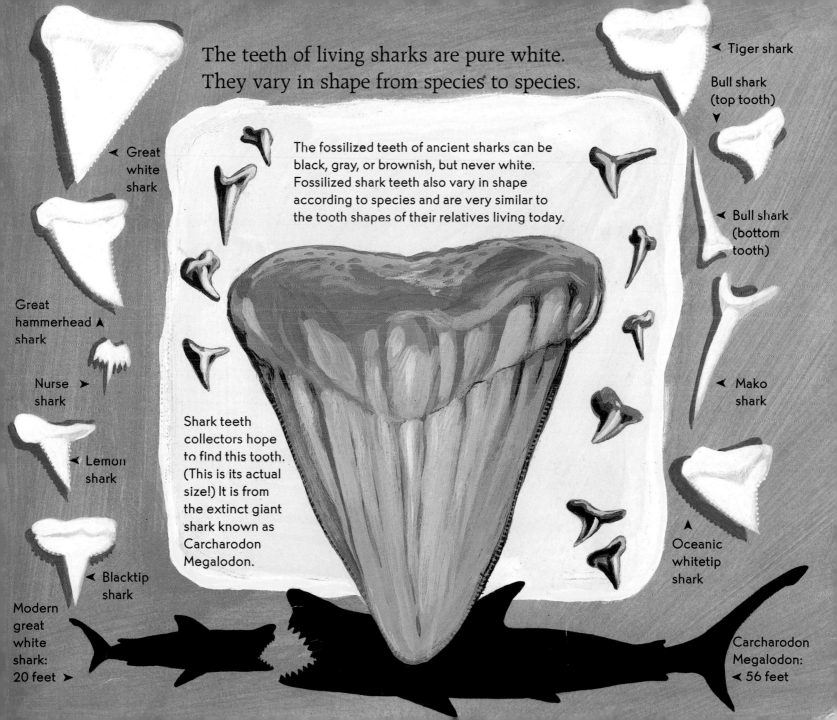

The teeth of living sharks are pure white.
They vary in shape from species to species.

The fossilized teeth of ancient sharks can be
black, gray, or brownish, but never white.
Fossilized shark teeth also vary in shape
according to species and are very similar to
the tooth shapes of their relatives living today.

◄ Tiger shark

Bull shark
(top tooth)
▼

◄ Bull shark
(bottom
tooth)

◄ Mako
shark

◄ Great
white
shark

Great
hammerhead ▲
shark

Nurse ➤
shark

Shark teeth
collectors hope
to find this tooth.
(This is its actual
size!) It is from
the extinct giant
shark known as
Carcharodon
Megalodon.

◄ Lemon
shark

◄ Blacktip
shark

Oceanic ▲
whitetip
shark

Modern
great
white
shark:
20 feet ➤

Carcharodon
Megalodon:
◄ 56 feet

Some species of sharks will occasionally travel in schools, but all sharks primarily hunt alone.

A school of hammerheads and several remoras

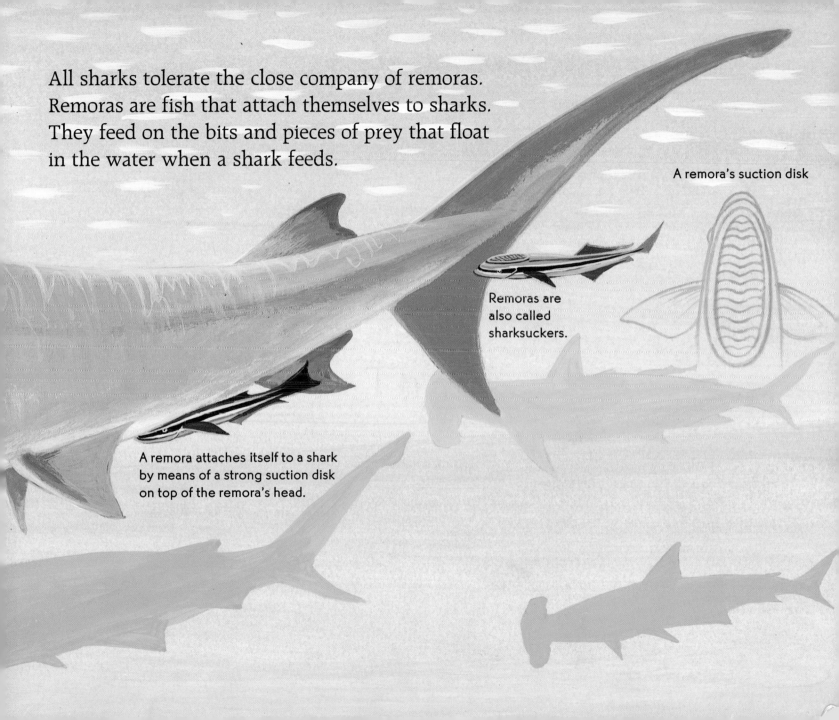

All sharks tolerate the close company of remoras.
Remoras are fish that attach themselves to sharks.
They feed on the bits and pieces of prey that float
in the water when a shark feeds.

A remora's suction disk

Remoras are
also called
sharksuckers.

A remora attaches itself to a shark
by means of a strong suction disk
on top of the remora's head.

Shark egg cases resemble tiny purses with long strings attached. Each egg-laying species produces its own type of egg case.

Horn shark egg case

Cat shark egg case

The case strings tangle in underwater weeds.

Sharks mate in shallow water where the male fertilizes eggs inside the female's body. Some shark species lay eggs. The female deposits the fertilized eggs amid underwater weeds and grasses. Each egg is inside a tough leathery egg case. Inside the case, a shark embryo is nourished by the egg yolk. When fully developed, a newborn shark breaks out of its egg case.

Shark embryo

Egg yolk

Some sharks' egg cases are transparent.

Dogfish shark egg case

Great hammerhead shark giving birth

Some shark species are live-bearers. The female gives birth to fully developed baby sharks. Each newborn shark is born tail first. All young sharks are called pups. A mother shark can give birth to up to 48 pups. From their first swim, shark pups must fend for themselves. All shark pups are miniature versions of their parents.

Tiger shark pup shown at half size

Young sharks eat mostly small fish and tiny shrimp.
Larger sharks eat larger fish, young sea turtles, and
floating birds. Great big sharks eat almost anything:
small fish, big fish, birds, sea otters, seals, sea turtles
of all sizes, dolphins, baby whales, swimming dogs,
people, and even each other.

Bottom-feeding sharks, such as the nurse shark, horn shark, and angel shark, feed on sea urchins, crabs, and lobsters. They vacuum up food from the ocean floor with their strong sucking mouths.

Red coral crab

Nurse shark

The largest sharks—whale sharks, basking sharks, and megamouth sharks—feed almost entirely on microscopic plankton. We are still learning about these mammoth sharks.

Whale shark

Cobia fish

We will learn more about all sharks as we overcome our fear and gain a better understanding of their life in the sea.